811
Gar

Gardner, John

A child's bestiary

DATE DUE

Anderson	JAN 23 '89		
NOV 3 '82	FEB 7 '89		
NOV 24 '82	MAR 10 '89		
JAN 3 '83	MAR 31 '89		
OCT 22 '85	Frankel		
FEB 13 '86	SEP 19 '89		
MAR 24 '87	MAR 20 '90		
APR 10 '87	APR 16 '90		
MAY 5 '87	SEP 27 '90		
JAN 8 '88	Douglas		
MAR 18 '88	MAR 6 '92		
NOV 23 '88			

A Child's
BESTIARY

Other books for young readers
by JOHN GARDNER

Dragon, Dragon
Gudgekin the Thistle Girl
The King of the Hummingbirds

A Child's
BESTIARY

BY
JOHN GARDNER

with additional poems by
Lucy Gardner &
Eugene Rudzewicz

&

drawings by
Lucy, Joel, Joan
& John Gardner

Alfred A. Knopf / *New York*

THIS IS A BORZOI BOOK PUBLISHED BY ALFRED A. KNOPF, INC.

Library of Congress Cataloging in Publication Data
Gardner, John Champlin, 1933-   A child's bestiary.
Summary: A collection of humorous verses about animals, friendly or otherwise. 1. Animals—Poetry. [1. Animals—Poetry] I. Title. PS3557.A712C5   811'.5'4   77-3945   ISBN 0-394-83483-6 ISBN 0-394-93483-0 Manufactured in the United States of America

For Betsy, John, and Sally

The Beasts

PAGE		PAGE	
2	The African Wild Dog	18	The Eagle
3	The Alligator	20	The Eel
4	The Armadillo	21	The Elephant
5	The Baboon	23	The Flying Squirrel
6	The Barracuda	24	The Frog
7	The Bear	25	The Garden Snake
8	The Beaver	25	The Gibbon
9	The Beefalo	27	The Giraffe
10	The Buzzard	28	The Gnat
11	The Camel	29	The Hippopotamus
13	The Cat & The Dog	30	The Hog-nosed Snake
13	The Chameleon	32	The House Mouse & The Church Mouse
14	The Cobra		
15	The Cockatoo	33	The Kangaroo
15	The Crab	34	The Leopard
16	The Crow	35	The Lion
17	The Duck	36	The Lizard

36   *The Lynx*

37   *The Mite*

38   *The Mole*

39   *The Mosquito*

39   *The Moth*

40   *The Musk Ox*

41   *The Octopus*

42   *The Opossum*

43   *The Owl*

44   *The Panther*

45   *The Peacock &*
      The Great Blue Heron

46   *The Penguin*

46   *The Phoenix*

47   *The Pig*

49   *The Python*

50   *The Red-headed*
      Woodpecker

51   *The Rhinoceros*

53   *The Shark*

54   *The Striped Hyena*

55   *The Swan*

56   *The Tiger*

57   *The Tree Toad &*
      The Three-toed Sloth

58   *The Turkey*

59   *The Turtle*

60   *The Walrus*

63   *The Wart Hog*

64   *The Wasp &*
      The Mud Dauber

64   *The Water Buffalo*

66   *The Whale*

66   *The Wolf*

67   *The Yeti*

68   *The Zebra*

Preface

A *Bestiary,* or Book of Beasts,
Is a thing full of high morality.
In the Middle Ages, such books were the rage.
If you can't find the moral, turn the page.

Introduction

Always be kind to animals,
Morning, noon, and night;
For animals have feelings too,
And furthermore, they bite.

A Child's
BESTIARY

The African Wild Dog

You ask for a civilized animal:
The African Wild Dog is one.
He hunts with a highly organized pack,
And after the work is done,

He takes back food to the young and the sick,
Those who could never, without him, survive;
And when some rival pack is harmed,
He keeps their young alive.

He lacks philosophy and art
But cleans himself and does what's right;
And he's religious in his way—
He barks at the moon at night.

The Alligator

When the Alligator opens his jaws
It gives people pause,
And they all step out of line
To read the sign,
Which says,

> VEGETARIAN
> WILL NOT EAT MEN

The people all nod to each other and smile
And say, "It isn't a Crocodile,
So obviously there is nothing at all to fear."
But they don't go near.

The Armadillo

The Armadillo
Is a queer fellow
Like a pig with a saddle
That's made from a turtle.
He digs
(As do pigs)
Or huddles
(Like turtles)
And he prays to heaven
For dirt to live in;
For unlike people (who are more complex),
He prays for nothing but what he expects.

The Baboon

Baboons, according to an article I read,
Drop rocks over cliffs when an enemy attacks.
This they do even (though it seems rather odd)
When it comes from above them and behind their backs.
Clearly their strategy doesn't always pay,
But why change a method you've got down pat?
Silly Baboon! —I'm sorry to say
There are people like that.

The Barracuda

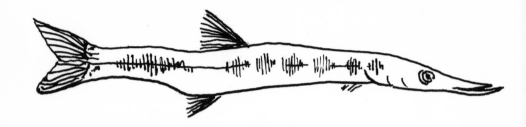

Slowly, slowly, he cruises,
And slowly, slowly, he chooses
Which kind of fish he prefers to take this morning;
Then without warning
The Barracuda opens his jaws, teeth flashing,
And with a horrible, horrible grinding and gnashing,
Devours a hundred poor creatures and feels no remorse.
It's no wonder, of course,
That no little fish much likes the thing,
And indeed, it occasionally strikes the thing,
That he really ought, perhaps, to change his ways.
"But," (as he says
With an evil grin)
"It's actually not my fault, you see:
I've nothing to do with the tragedy;
I open my mouth for a yawn and—ah me!—
They all
        swim
              in."

The Bear

If somebody offers you a Bear, bow low
And say no.

The Beaver

When the trees the Beaver requires for his dam
Are too far away from the Beaver's stream,
He cuts down the trees with his sawblade teeth,
Trims off the branches, catches his breath,
Saws the tree up into four-foot bits,
Looks the pile over and uses his wits:
He digs a canal about two feet wide,
Pushes the sawed logs over the side,
And floats them down to where the dam's to be.
Tell me a cleverer beast than he!

The Beefalo

The Beefalo is a bison and a cow
Blended together, God knows how.
He's a human creation, entirely new,
Made by a scientist. God knows who.
Hooray for humanity! Well may we strut!
We're *some animal*! God knows what.

The Buzzard

When people see the Buzzard in the sky
They commonly shudder and wonder why
He's there, and they shudder again and say,
"Go away!"

Every time they see the Buzzard
They shudder;
And every time his name comes up in conversation,
In whatever connection,
They shudder.

Now a Buzzard's like anyone else in that
He doesn't like being shuddered at.
And therefore, when he isn't searching
For a meal, he spends long hours perching,
Sunk in gloom,
Like an Angel of Doom,
On a lonely rock-cliff high in the night,
Out of sight.

The Camel

God and the Son and Muhammad the Prince,
With the help of Shiva and Quetzalcoatl,
Decided to work as a group for once
And invent the beautiful Camel.

The Son gave him grace like a bird in flight;
Shiva, who had his own opinions,
Twisted his brain up and taught him to bite
And scented his breath with onions.

Muhammad provided a mountain for his back
To give him comfort in every land;
Quetzalcoatl, on a sacrifice kick,
Made feet that worked best on sand.

God filled the mountain with water and food
And gave him big eyelids, in case of wind;
And when they had finished, the gods all stood
And looked at the creature and grinned.

Along came Buddha. Said the gods in delight,
"You can't make a Holy One of *this* beast, child!"
Buddha considered. "He seems all right
As he is," he said, and smiled.

The Cat & The Dog

Though he purrs, the Cat's only partly here,
Poised between the hearth and the street outside.
Half tame, half wild, he's a walking riddle,
Playing both ends against the middle.
And so man hangs between Truths he must fear
And the murderous animal under his hide.
The Dog's by nature the best of his friends,
Playing the middle against both ends.

The Chameleon

People say the Chameleon can take the hue
Of whatever he happens to be on. It's true
—Within reason, of course. If you put him on plaid
Or polka dots, he gets really mad.

The Cobra

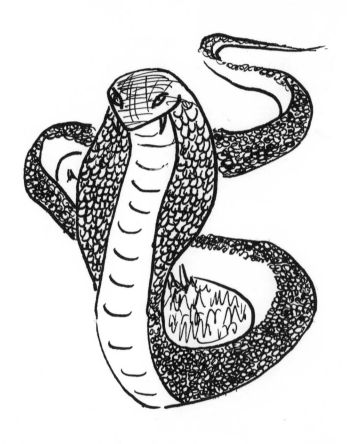

Like a king, the Cobra lifts
His hooded, terrifying head.
"The facts are so-and-so," says he,
And quicker than lightning, all agree.
And then he'll sway and hypnotize
Till even those most swift, most wise,
Are helpless against his venomed tooth.
They might as well have told the truth.

The Cockatoo

The Cockatoo is widely known
For talking on the telephone
And also (wretched, thoughtless bird)
For hanging up without a word.

The Crab

Never grab a Crab.

The Crow

"The first thing to know,"
Said God to the Crow,
" (If you want to get on,
And make points with my Son)
Is: If you steal things
(Gum wrappers, rings)
Be quick! be sly!
And if possible, try
To give fair exchange.
As for the range
Of your voice, keep it low,
For vulgarity, Crow,
Reflects on me.
By my works I'm known,
And, alas, you're one.
Go easy on gardens;
Don't tease shotguns . . .
What else should I say?
Chitchat's O.K.

But when the whole flock's aroun'
Try to keep it down.
Be considerate, ye know?
In general, Crow,
Don't be a dope.
Imitate the Pope."

"The first thing to know,"
Said the Son to the Crow,
"Is: Try not to be
Too disgusting, see?
But *celebrate,* you know?
Like I mean: Be a Crow."

The Duck

The Duck
Has pluck.
He's a brawler.

A Duck
Is good luck,
Unless you're smaller.

The Eagle

When the Eagle glides over, the land grows still;
Not a mouse dares squeak, not a songbird sings,
Not even the horses in the field speak out,
Awed by the shadow of wings.
Even the man by the road grows still,
One, for the moment, with the shivering mouse,
Till the shadow of motionless wings glides on
And the world creeps back to its house.

I spoke with an old sick Eagle at the zoo
Confined in a cage so that children might see
What Eagles are. His feathers drooped,
He was hunched up with misery.
"There's been," said the Eagle, "some ghastly mistake.
This shabby old creature with the rheumy eye,
This is no Eagle! My noblest part
Is silence and the sudden sky."

The Eel

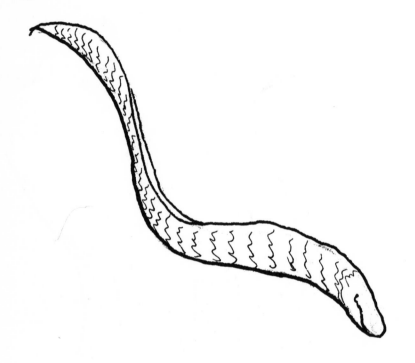

When people feel
Of an Eel,
They cry, "Oh!"
And, "Well, well!"
And, "I say!"
And the Eel who has shocked them so
Gives a quiet little smile
And swims away.

The Elephant

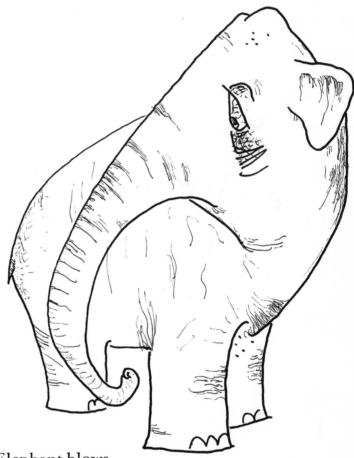

When the Elephant blows
His nose,
All the people stand back,
And the elephant-keeper exclaims,
"Give him room! Give him room!"
"Is he going to do it?" the people all shout.
"He *may*," says the elephant-keeper.
"You'd better watch out!"
A hush falls over the zoo

And the city too,
And the great, gray trunk lifts,
And the Elephant glances about, and sniffs,
And the people all lend him their handkerchiefs . . .
And then it comes:
KER-BOOM! KER-BOOM! KER-BOOOOM!
The handkerchiefs fly
Till they blot out the sky
And everywhere in the park people cry,
"Why, it's dark! It's dark!
It's only five o'clock, and the whole park's dark!"
The elephant-keeper chuckles and looks small:
"The Elephant's blowing his nose again, that's all."

When the Elephant blows
His nose,
Everything goes!

The Flying Squirrel

The Flying Squirrel is crazy.
Though he has no feathers (much less wings),
He scampers up into the tallest tree
And cries, "Toot-toot! I'm a parachute!"
And away off the highest branches he springs
Into empty air, spreading every hair,
His arms and legs flung wide to each side,
Till he lands with a thump that's almost quiet . . .

Admire it, child, but don't try it.

The Frog

The Frog sits succulent on his lily pad:
Buddha-like, not bad,
He snaps up gnats
Between his juicy jaws.

In summer dusk
He croaks
Like jokes
Played on a cello.
As dusk grows dim, his mating song grows mellow.

His back is slimy green,
His bloated bellows velvet yellow.
In restaurants,
By candlelight,
Some lovers think there's no more tasty fellow.

(E. W. R.)

24

The Garden Snake

"Higgledy piggledy tongue-flicking Garden Snake
Why have you made our poor grandmother faint?"
"When she came picking up kindling and firewood,
She reached for me, and I ain't."

The Gibbon

The Gibbon, as you can tell by his manner,
Is a planner.
He has long, long lists of Things to Do
Which he never gets through;
When he darts into one thing he has in mind,
He remembers another
And gets in a dither
And falls farther and farther behind
Till at last he sits down, dejected, by the wall
And nibbles his knuckles and peeps
And does nothing at all.

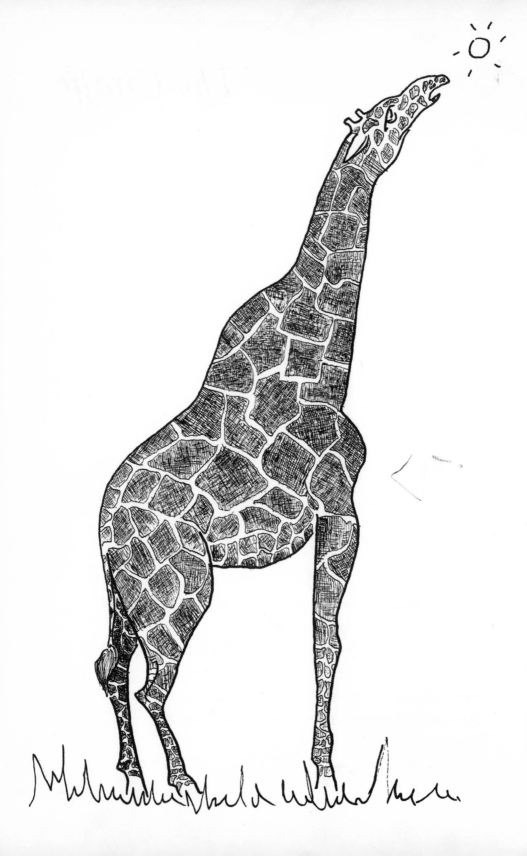

The Giraffe

The Giraffe precariously tilts
On short and long stilts.
And his neck is long
And thoroughly wrong;
But does the Giraffe curl up in a corner
And curse his lot
And regret that he's not
Attractive?
And do people say, "Nothing could look forlorner?"
No sir, not at all! He's active!
He stretches his neck up and munches the sun,
And then, whenever he takes the notion,
He's off like a windmill in slow-motion;
And people throw their hands in the air
And cry, "I declare!
See him *RUN*!"

The Gnat

Gnats are gnumerous
But small.
We hardly gnotice them
At all.

(E. W. R.)

The Hippopotamus

Regard the Hippopotamus,
    For he is very wise:
He does not work and slave like us
    But lives on cakes and pies
And other sweets, and grows immense,
    And when his legs collapse,
He rolls himself into the swamps
    And floats and licks his chops.

Regard the Hippopotamus,
    For he is very wise:
He does not work and slave like us
    But lives! on cakes and pies.

The Hog-nosed Snake or
"Hog Snake"

The hog-nosed snake is the chief exponent of the art of acting among snakes. Although without fangs, poison, or a constricting capacity, and comparatively small (though exceedingly fat), it can, by flattening its head and neck and hissing, make itself appear almost as ferocious as the most dreaded cobras of the Old World. When molested, it will coil its tail, raise its head, and, taking a deep breath in perfect imitation of a venomous species, spread its hood to almost three times its normal size. Hissing loudly, it begins to strike, though it cannot be induced to bite.

If it finds its assailant undaunted by the tactics of the cobra or puff-adder, it switches to the tactics of a boa constrictor or, if need be, a silent rattlesnake.

Nor is this all. If pugnacious tactics fail to ward off danger, it will resort to the opposite course, and simulate death as though suddenly struck down by the mere threat of danger before it. It opens its mouth, goes into convulsions until exhausted, then rolls over on its back as though dead. Vigorous handling, moreover, while in this state will produce no sign of life in the snake. The only flaw in the show is that the snake has learned its lesson too well, for when placed on its abdomen it will immediately roll over on its back again as though this were the only position suitable to the dead.*

* *American Wild Life, Illustrated,* compiled by the Writers' Program of the Works Project Administration in the City of New York (W. M. Wise & Co., Inc., New York, 1947, pp. 373–74).

The House Mouse &
The Church Mouse

The House Mouse lives upon crackers and cheese;
The Church Mouse lives on *Ecclesiastes*.
The House Mouse's life is all song and laughter;
The Church Mouse will gather his crackers hereafter.

The Kangaroo

The Kangaroo is of course by nature
An earth-bound creature.
Swallows may soar and dive in the wind,
Wide-winged hawks may circle the sun,
And the owl may sit in the crescent moon,
For creatures with wings
Are designed for such things;
But the Kangaroo is forever bound
To the ground.
Now naturally, given the way he's made,
The Kangaroo ought to sit in the shade
And munch tender grasses and try to find
Great thoughts to occupy his mind;
But the Kangaroo is somewhat queer:
He bounds and pounces and leaps in the air,
And he tries . . .
And he tries . . .
And he tries . . .
And he flies!

The Leopard

The Leopard, animal trainers say,
Is remarkably like you and me.
Though lions happily work in teams,
The height of a spotted Leopard's dreams
Is to work alone, just the trainer and he.

Work him alone, the trainer says,
And you'd hardly believe he has razor-sharp claws.
He's a beautiful creature, he wants you to know.
He smiles and purrs, "I'm the Star of the Show!
See how my man puts his head in my jaws!"

But bring six other leopards on
And the Leopard's heart turns suddenly stone.
He snaps at the whip and refuses to crawl
And swipes at the trainer, as if to bawl,
"I've told you and told you, I work *alone*!"

He'll happily leap through hoops of flame
Or sit up and beg on a painted drum.
Ask him to work with his brothers and sisters,
And his heart recoils and swells and blisters
And he leaps out to slash you to Kingdom Come.

But life does not go as the Leopard would wish.
However his furious tail may swish,
The whip-crack insists on the act as a whole;
So the Leopard grumbles but plays his role,
And the trainer says "*Good* boy!" and fills his dish.

34

The Lion

The old father Lion
Is a male chauvinist pig.
His wives don't much like it,
But listen: he's *big*.

It's no use reasoning;
His eyes merely glaze.
He's stupid, like people,
In the good old days.

The Lizard

The Lizard is a timid thing
That cannot dance or fly or sing;
He hunts for bugs beneath the floor
And longs to be a dinosaur.

The Lynx

The Lynx
Thinks
He's a fighting whiz,
Which he is.

The Lynx
Thinks
He's cunning, too,
Which is true.

The Lynx
Thinks
We're *nothing* like that,
So we gang up and shoot the ridiculous cat.

The Mite

The Mite
Might choose
To dangle on a widow's ear
Like a penny bauble.
Then again,
He might not.
    (E. W. R.)

The Mole

Three cheers for the Mole
Who lives in a hole
And never complains
If it snows or rains!
One can't help feeling he's clever
To sit in his house
Curled up like a mouse,
And to never
(Or anyway almost never)
Come up for a thoughtful look at the weather.
"Don't look," says he,
"And you'll never see
That the weather's grim."
Three cheers for him!

The Mosquito

Let us sing praise of the bold and determined Mosquito,
Kamakazi of the insect world, who strikes
As bravely as they did once for Hirohito;
Nothing can drive him off, but again and again
He dives in the name of the only good he knows.
For though his goal is less than that of those
Who died for love—with silk scarves trailing, white,
Roaring into fiery death for their fellow men—
He honors life in his way. At their high whim,
The gods can make a buddha of even him.

The Moth

In the absence of mothballs, the Moth
Eats cloth.
It makes people yell,
But it seems just as well.
Who wants a cloth with a mothball smell?

The Musk Ox

When somebody threatens the Musk Ox herd
They gather in a circle, without a word,
With the cows and the young inside, protected,
Till the threat, whatever it is, is deflected.
They're no great fighters; they merely defend
Their weak and their young—or some human friend.
The hunter, with his gun and bullet boxes,
Thinks he's smarter than the old Musk Ox is.
When he grows stiff and shrivels like a gnome
His family sends him to the old folks' home.

The Octopus

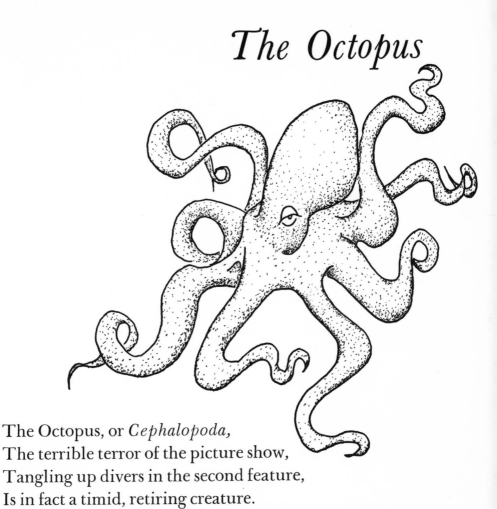

The Octopus, or *Cephalopoda*,
The terrible terror of the picture show,
Tangling up divers in the second feature,
Is in fact a timid, retiring creature.

He's scary to look at, but never attacks,
Just huddles in caves among underwater rocks,
And if he's discovered, he's too scared to think
But clouds up the water with great swirls of ink

And scuttles away in an eight-legged hurry
To some other cave, where he sits full of worry
And hopes no one finds him, with which I agree.
If someone *must* find him, I hope it's not me.

The Opossum

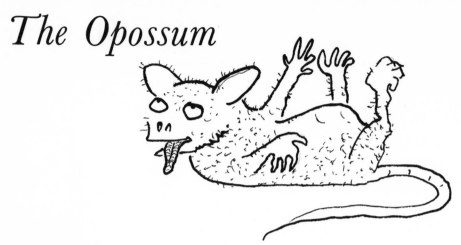

One day, having nothing much to do, God
Created the Opossum. It was a kind of experiment:
How stupid, ugly, and downright odd
A creature (he wondered) could he possibly invent?
When the 'Possum was created, God shook his head
And grinned. "That's not very good," he said.

But for no real reason he liked the fool thing
And kept the thing functioning age after age.
The dinosaurs died out, or began to sing,
Transformed into birds; apes became the rage;
But the 'Possum trudged on—with some other antiques:
Spiders, sand-crabs, various old freaks.

"Father," said the Son, "that 'Possum's a killer—
Murders baby chicks for no reason. He's got to go!
Times have changed, and changed for the better.
He's an anachronism, if I may say so."
God sighed. "Peace and Justice are right," he said,
And whispered to the 'Possum: "Lie down. Play dead."

The Owl

In broad daylight,
Inferior sight
Has the Owl;
And so, when the poor old fowl
Forgets, for some reason, to fly to his tree
At night (which is when he is able to see),
He's forced to perch in whatever is near,
And for miles and miles around people hear
His cries of "Hooo! Boo-hooo!"
The other birds, of course, hear it too,
And they cock their heads and stop their song
And hurry over to see what's wrong.
The crow says, "Haw!" and the woodpecker says,
        "Tut, tut!"
And the hummingbird says, "Hmmm. He's off his nut!"
They jeer and chortle and say with a look of surprise,
"Him they call wise!"
The Owl sits, glum, and he hears them run on and on,
And he tries to convey the impression he's
        deaf as a stone;
But at last—at last!—the sun sinks
And the Owl blinks
And slowly discovers that now he can see again.
Then
He goes stumbling and mumbling and grumbling
        and terribly depressed
To his nest.

The Panther

Lock your doors when the Panther roars,
Especially after dark,
For you can't hear his feet as he moves down the street
Or lopes across the park.

He's black as the night, but his eyes are bright—
His eyes, which are all you can see:
They burn like coals as the Panther strolls
In the dark of the shrubbery.

The Panther has got a stone for a heart:
He would eat his own mother or niece;
So lock your doors when the Panther roars,
And telephone the police!

The Peacock &
The Great Blue Heron

The handsomest creature in all the zoo
Is the Peacock; however, he scarcely knows it.
He drags his tail through the duck manure,
And it shows it.
The ugliest creature, on the other hand,
Is the Great Blue Heron. But from his point of view,
He's smarter and nobler and far more grand
Than you.

The Penguin

The Penguin is often compared, wrongly,
To a gentleman in a tuxedo.
The Penguin is all good taste and charm,
The Man, all drunken libido.

The Phoenix

There's only one Phoenix in the world at a time.
After its thousand-year life span passes
It settles in its nest and explodes into flame
And rises again from its own same ashes.
Cynics deny this—unreasonably.
 (It might be different if I said there are three.)

The Pig

The Pig, according to the ancient Celts,
Could understand the wind,
And knew the gods by their first names
And suffered when he sinned.

Alas, how fallen is the Pig
Who wallows now in mire
For all his keen intelligence
And preternatural fire!

He grunts and feeds and grows more fat
And fills with filth his sty;
How trifling his ambitions are!
How dim his tiny eye!

One evening walking near a beach
Littered and mostly dead,
I met a Pig with the gift of speech,
And this is what he said:

"Mankind, according to ancient Pigs,
Could understand the wind,
And knew the gods by their first names
And suffered when he sinned.

"Alas, how fallen is mankind
Who wallows now in trash,
For all his keen intelligence,
His fire cooled to ash!"

The Python

One afternoon, while sitting in a tree,
God thought up the Python.
He cracked a grin and clapped his hands
And at once got down and made one.

When the Son came by, the Python hissed
When the Son only meant to touch him.
"He's a wonderful kind of snake," said the Son,
"But if I was you, I'd watch him."

The Python from then on did nothing wrong
Till in Eden trouble came,
And Adam and Eve swore up and down
That the Python was to blame.

All Heaven had doubts, but the Python was cleared
By a full investigation;
Yet no one has trusted a Python since.
Beware of a bad reputation.

The Red-headed Woodpecker

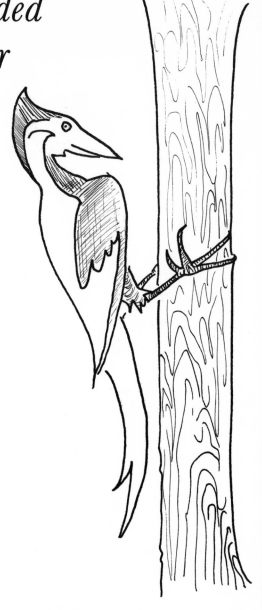

"Higgledy piggledy Red-headed Woodpecker,
Why are you pecking that hole in my tree?"
"I think I hear savory insects inside, but
With all this damn wood I can't see!"

The Rhinoceros

Rhinoceroses are grumpy:
They keep to themselves, and they'll tell you their reasons
    bluntly.
If someone tries to be friends,
The Rhinoceros frumps,
And thumps,
And lowers his two-horned snout
And seems put out,
And there, more often than not, the matter ends.

Rhinoceroses are grumpy:
When a Rhinoceros has a party,
He invites all the other Rhinoceroses, and if and when
    they come,

He
Stands around looking glum
And takes exception to everything they say,
And so do they,
Until, with a furious toss of their snouts and a last
        snort of gloom,
They all flounce home.

The Shark

The Shark is a trifle crazy.
   Whenever he goes for a swim,
The people all give him a glance askance
   And say, "What's bothering *him*?"
And when the Shark goes visiting,
   Down under the waves and the foam,

His friends see him coming and bolt their doors
And bury their valuables under their floors
And hide all their children in dresser drawers,
   And pretend they're not at home.

The Shark, as I mentioned, is crazy,
   And when he takes the air,
And hurries toward where he's noticed a crowd,
   There's never anyone there.
And when the Shark has a birthday,
   No party is thrown for the Shark
Unless, of course, he throws his own,
In which case he winds up the gramophone
And plays "Happy Birthday" and sits alone
   Eating his cake in the dark.

The Striped Hyena

The Striped Hyena never combs his hair
And has no idea what's hidden there,
Such as lice or mice,
Termites, cockroaches, grubs, nits, chickens—
I say, Hooray! After all—what the dickens?—
If human beings can make a zoo,
Why not him too?

54

The Swan

The Swan is an ancient symbol of the human soul.
To the casual eye, she's elegant and lazy,
Borne on the stream as if by Grace.
But she's paddling like crazy.

The Tiger

The Tiger is a perfect saint
As long as you respect him;
But if he happens to say *ain't*,
You'd better not correct him.

The Treetoad &
The Three-toed Sloth

The Tree Toad and the Three-toed Sloth
Are both tree-dwelling creatures,
And both have ugly, albeit dissimilar, features,
And both move very slowly, if at all,
And never fall.
You would think that, having so much in common,
    they'd be
The best of friends, and would live in the same tree;
But not at all.
When the Tree Toad and the Three-toed Sloth
Happen to meet, they both froth
At the mouth, and glower, and hurriedly back off.

The Turkey

The Turkey's so dumb he can drown in the rain;
Revive the poor creature, he'll do it again.

He wouldn't approve of Thanksgiving, no doubt;
If the Turkey was able to figure it out.

But he doesn't think twice, he just eats and gets fat,
And along comes the axman and, well sir, that's that.

We needn't feel guilty or sniffle or wince;
If it wasn't for us, he'd have died out long since.

It's Man's tender care that makes Turkeys thrive;
If we'd eaten the dodo he'd still be alive.

The Turtle

Beware the murdering Turtle,
You ducklings in the stream:
For while you paddle and quirtle,
He's nearer than you dream!

He's down in the ooze of the riverbed
Among tires and boots and old tin,
And if he should notice you overhead,
You'd never be noticed again.

The Walrus
(An Evolutionary Tale)

The thoughtful old Walrus with the mournful eyes
once lived on land. But times were hard;
there was drought in his country,
    and animals more fierce
kept chasing him, frightening his children,
    until one day he was fed up completely and
—his mind wandering while he said his prayers—

he got the idea
of withdrawing with his family to the sea.
"Others," he observed to God, "have done it.
The whale, I might mention, has lumbered down
from land to the ocean, to work on his singing
(an excellent musician).
The porpoise, I might add, has abandoned hard ground,
fulfilling himself as a water-person,
chattering all day, telling cuttlefish jokes,
in times of shipwreck rushing to man's aid,
or the aid of any cow or horse aboard,
nudging the half-drowned creature back to shore.
And the seal's done it. I could make him my puppy."
"Try it!" said God, "That's what *I'd* do! Why not?"
Always alert to new inventions,
He thought about talking the donkey into going to sea.

The thoughtful old Walrus, brooding on his troubles,
announced his decision
(originally, though he forgot, it was his wife's decision),
bid ponderous and sad farewell to the land
and slipped with his family into the kingdom of the Fish.
("He's crazy," the Son said, "—but that's all right,
      that's all right!
Good luck, you crazy Walrus!")
It was a world as strange as the American West
to those who moved across the prairies
      in covered wagons,
a world alarming and inhospitable, at first,
but beautiful, in its way. Little by little,

with noisy encouragement but not much practical help
        from the Father and Son,
the Walrus and his family got the hang of it;
they became good swimmers, learned ways to deal
with the dangers of the sea, such as sharks and storms,
found rocky places where they could crawl back,
        now and again,
        to rest.

One day the Father and Son went to visit.
The Walrus sat in his moustache, gazing out to sea,
his tusks like the tusks of his cousin the elephant,
watching men's ships, seeing how they steamed across
        the water to war,
how they slaughtered whole choirs of whales
        to make supper
        and perfumes . . .
"I don't understand it," he said.
        "Why do we put up with it?"
"Don't worry, I have a plan," God said,
        and looked crafty.
"Faddle," said the Son. "All we have is time."
"That's my plan!" God said.
        (He'd weasel out of anything.)
        "Given time enough,
even this crazy crackpot Man
may come to understand he's one of us."

The Wart Hog

Oh do not bring the Wart Hog here!
The Wart Hog is a name I fear.
He may be moderately bright
But his temper's foul, and he's a sight.
Oh, do not bring the Wart Hog here,
Take him to Troy or Rensselaer!

The Wasp &
The Mud Dauber

The Wasp will die for his clan without thought,
As noble a fighter as God ever wrought.
When we're the enemy, we mind his ways,
But in terms of the hive, such courage pays.

The Mud Dauber, though he may first appear
Much like the Wasp, prefers to stay clear
Of relatives; he shuns his clan
And lives all alone like a crazyman.
But something's to be said for solitary things.
The Mud Dauber sulks, but he never stings.

The Water Buffalo

In Southeast Asia, when you go,
You'll meet the Water Buffalo.
It's more or less a common cow
A farmer can milk or hitch to a plow
Or ride (although it's very slow
Traveling by Water Buffalo).

Allowed to do as he might please
He'd stand all day in water to his knees
And switch his tail or rub his hump
On trees at the edge of the jungle swamp.
But no such luck; work bends him low,
This poor old Water Buffalo.

And yet you won't hear him complain.
Religion's dim in the old beast's brain,
But he remembers what Buddha said
And does what's right. After he's dead
He'll rise to a better life, he knows,
Than a poor old Water Buffalo's.

The Whale

Have you heard the Whale sing?
He can sing like anything!
Science has the sound on tape
(Together with the talking ape).

Whales are grandiosely large,
Larger than an ocean barge,
Larger than an ocean liner,
Even aeroplanes are tinier.

The largest animal there is
Is perfectly content with his
Diet of greens—he takes no prey.
Still, take care when he comes to play.
      (L. G.)

The Wolf

The Wolf is a very good watchdog, it's true;
The only trouble is,
He considers all he protects, and you too,
His.

The Yeti

The Yeti is a manlike beast,
Unless, perchance, he doesn't exist.
He walks like a man and has hair on his face,
And rumors persist
That in forests and caves where no one goes,
Or high in the Himalayan snows,
He may still be living. Nobody knows.
If you meet him and ask him, "Are you a Yeti?"
All he can say is, "Maybe."

The Zebra

The Zebra is of course
A horse
Of sorts;
However, he is not to be confused
With those sorts of horses that are used
For riding or for pulling a sleigh
Or bringing in hay;
For though a horse of sorts, he has his
Certain little preferences:
He won't be made to work, and if you try,
The Zebra smiles and looks sly
And finds some stripes of shadow and sits down
And seems to disappear into the ground.
But don't be fooled. Shout, "Hey, are you asleep, huh?"
And if the shadows snore, well, that's the Zebra.

The End

Such are the lessons we learn from the beasts,
Unless at some point I'm mistaken;
Nature's abundant, there's gods in the trees,
And you, child, will not be forsaken.

The Poets and the Artists

from left: Eugene Rudzewicz, Joan, Lucy, John, and Joel Gardner

Photo by Boskydell Artists, Ltd.

A Note About John Gardner

John Gardner won the hearts and minds of a whole genera-
tion of young readers with his first books for children, three
collections of original fairy tales: *The King of the Hum-
mingbirds, Gudgekin the Thistle Girl,* and *Dragon, Dragon.*
His highly acclaimed adult novels include *The Wreckage
of Agathon, Grendel, The Sunlight Dialogues, Nickel
Mountain,* and *October Light,* winner of the 1976 National
Book Critics Circle Award for Fiction. Since 1958 he has
taught medieval literature at several universities and has
published a highly praised biography, *The Life and Times
of Geoffrey Chaucer,* as well as translations of *The Com-
plete Works of the Gawain Poet* and *The Alliterative Morte
Arthure and Other Poems from Middle English.* He has
also written many articles on medieval literature for schol-
arly journals. Mr. Gardner was born in 1933 in Batavia,
New York.